The

SEA AMONG

the

CUPBOARDS

POEMS BY MAUREEN SEATON

Selected by Jean Valentine as the
1989 Capricorn Poetry Prize Winner

NEW RIVERS PRESS

1992

Edited by C. W. Truesdale
Editorial Assistance by Paul J. Hintz
Cover painting by Louise Williams
Book Design and Typesetting by Peregrine Publications

The Sea among the Cupboards was the 1989 Winner of the Capricorn Poetry Prize, spo
sored by the Writer's Voice, a program of the Westside YMCA's Center for the Arts
New York City. This selection was made by Jean Valentine.

The publication of *The Sea among the Cupboards* has been made possible by grants fro
the Arts Development Fund of the United Arts Council, the First Bank System Found
tion, Liberty State Bank, the Star Tribune/Cowles Media Company, the Tennant Cor
pany Foundation, and the National Endowment for the Arts (with funds appropriate
by the Congress of the United States). New Rivers Press also wishes to acknowled
the Minnesota Non-Profits Assistance Fund for its invaluable support.

New Rivers Press books are distributed by

The Talman Company
150 Fifth Avenue
New York, NY 10011

Bookslinger
2402 University Avenue We
Saint Paul, MN 55114

The Sea among the Cupboards has been manufactured in the United States of Ameri
for New Rivers Press, 420 N. 5th Street/Suite 910, Minneapolis, MN 55401 in the
first edition of 1,400 copies.

For Jennifer and Emily

ACKNOWLEDGEMENTS

Grateful acknowledgement is made to the following publications in which some of these poems first appeared: *Cottonwood, Croton Review, Downtown, Ikon, The Iowa Review, The Madison Review, Mississippi Review, The Missouri Review, Negative Capability, New Letters, Plainsong, Poetry East, Poet Lore, Poetry Northwest, Rhino,* and *The Widener Review.*

The author wishes to thank her family in Illinois and New Jersey, with special thanks to Marialice Seaton. And for their invaluable support during the writing of this book—Patricia Farewell, H. P., and Ruth Lisa Schechter, in fond memory.

CONTENTS

CLOISTER

MORTAL SINS

Aldo Palmieri straddles
the back seat of the schoolbus,
chainsmokes Luckys like a cowboy.
I'm fifteen.
I love his pathos, his acne,
his yellow-stained fingers.
JFK dies during study hall.
Jane Murphy gets pregnant, leaves
school. I take phenobarbital daily
for my nerves.

At sixteen my face falls into place
around my nose.
I meet Harvey Brotman underwater
at the Jones Beach pool.
We share whoppers with cheese in Franklin Square.
His parents say: "One date with a Catholic
girl is too much."
I think Harvey is making this up.

I'm seventeen:
long hair, brace-less teeth.
I worship Kevin Duffy, boast
his fraternity pin
on my Peter Pan collar.
I think kissing is a mortal sin.
I think holding hands is possibly
a mortal sin.
Father Reilly says: "Watch out! Holding hands
is a venial that could easily lead
to a mortal."
Kevin drops me for a "Popover Girl" from Patricia Murphy's
who giggles whenever a car with one headlight
passes by.

3

I meet my husband-to-be at the Ship Ahoy
in New Rochelle, acquire a taste for scotch;
at eighteen, trade eternity
for a good french kiss.
I learn to cook Thanksgiving dinner
for twenty in-laws, put on weight,
take it off, put it on, learn
my husband prefers blondes.

I'm thirty-one:
the year of designer jeans.
My ass is finally "in."
I get my ears double-pierced,
cut six inches off my hair, let it grow
on my legs, under my arms.
I take my daughter to the Twin Towers.
We look down, say "Wow."
She holds my face in her baby hands,
says: "You're so pretty, Mommy."
I laugh.
She tells me again & again
until one day, I am.

THE FIRST DRINK

My mother stands in the doorway,
always leaving. She thinks
I'm a woman. Her face shows this –
how odd. I'm four years old
or less. The scene: Grandma's
kitchen, my father, his lap, me.
The choice: him or her. My heart
empties soundlessly. I need her
but she never touches me.
The kitchen seems to shrink when she leaves
like some hot air balloon dying.

Objects take on life like that:
street signs, trees. I hear everything
scream. I'm careful with everything.
The piano hurts when I touch it.
The glass angel feels lonely
when I leave the room. I can't bear
the cries of animals or babies.
I'm seven years old, careful
not to crease my communion dress
or bite the body of Christ. When they
say the word sin, I believe them.

Late October: I bleed for the first time,
ruin my Halloween costume.
I want to lay my head in my father's
lap, absorb his equilibrium,
but he thinks I'm a woman now,
screams at me to cover myself. His fear
is an undertow that drags him away. The years
grow between us like bad children.

5

I spend reckless weekends
before an eternal candle and gilded wafer
they call God, starve my flesh
to fine points, hard planes.
At sixteen, the first drink goes down
like a flame: purifying, hot.
I feel the answers flood my toes,
the promise seize my brain
like sunlight in a corner of hell.

THE LAKESHORE LIMITED

She's terrified of movement, trains
that shatter the night with speed.

Topaz lights connect the black shores
of the Hudson, startle her, slouched
in the window seat.

The train moves forward on wheels
of desperation: muffled rock, primitive
drumbeat. She changes her name
to Kate. For eighteen hours,
she assumes an identity of adventure.

She meets a boy with bloodshot eyes
caught in the maze of a hangover. "Why,"
he says, "do I drink as if death
held relief?" He believes in reincarnation.
He hopes he's an old soul.

They sleep together in an empty sleeper
through Toledo and the lonely cornfields
of Indiana. As they leave Eastern Standard

she tells him her name is Kate,
and he believes her.

OVER EGGS

And Dad I said, because she begged me,
she's due in August and she plans
to keep the baby. Dad?

One familiar vein rose purple
near his right eye.

He swallowed a bite of toast,
blurted something about the father:
did she know for sure who it was?

Of course, I sniffed; threw the name
like a knife at his throat.

He winced.
The yolk oozed slowly over my plate,
making me suddenly sick.

When I hug her now, I feel the child growing,
a sword beneath her breast.

RICKY'S AMERICA

With a few blasts under her belt
Maggie curls up contentedly in your lap
and makes you moan. Forget Jim
she says and you do
until the three of you wake up thirsty
around noon, twisted together like pretzels
on the kitchen floor, covering your nakedness
with leftover cocaine and a cup of Catawba
for breakfast. Your family steps over you
on their way back from church, asks politely
would your friends like fresh bagels
or some eggs? Maggie chugs another beer
as you forget her name and loosen your belt.
Watch her blue eyes float as she goes down
for the third time.

NO TALKING

Two adults at table.
Cigar smoke drifts.
My mother has tears
on her face. The other
is my father.

No talking.

Daddy prefers issues,
knows everything.
He calls us "gals"
as if we smelled of laundry,
says: When you gals find
something worth talking about
I'll sit down and listen.

No talking.

I hyperspace to other planets.
I've been chosen by God.
This is your little girl
signing off from Saturn where
the rings would make your
head spin —

They never leave, they leave me
alone; hold martinis
near their smiles, smile
at thin air. Their pain
seeps into green carpets,
lodges in my throat
like a jagged bone.

Tonight I saw lightning
beyond the Tappan Zee:
hot flashes from other worlds.
In my mouth: the ashes of some
fidelity, one small flame.

THE LOST FATHER

You materialize from the '60s.
We're both tipsy, both thirty-two.
We laugh at your crew-cut while
I hide the fact that I've been
nearly raped, that my near-assailant
was deterred by the sight of menstrual blood.

In your usual way, you can't afford
to care. I know this, but my life
remains a cliché of expectation.
As a child, I rescued worms
from hot suburban sidewalks. You worked

somewhere in the Bronx or Staten Island.
We had two dates when I was twelve:
Camelot and Bye Bye Birdie. Age thirteen
threw a knife between us, stained my legs
the color of cheap wine.

I'm afraid you'll die drunk on Avenue D.
You tell me, never mind. A rat
the size of Jersey slithers by.
After a good rain, those worms could drive me
crazy, stranded on the pavement
like soldiers with their legs blown off.
By noon they'd be dried out and dead.
Hundreds of them. Never enough time.

In the '80s, you swear you'll never drink again.
I stare at the phone in my hand while
the sun bows behind the Palisades. I say:
The rapist was a man I'd known for years;
I lied about the blood.

PECULIAR SEASON

Your breasts are small, close to your body
with perfect brown nipples. When I touch you,
I'm amazed at the calm in your face.

I remember the shade pulled down, street sounds
through chinks of light, the smell of bleach,
"Love of Life" coming on, going off.

You slipped quickly into magic. It trans-
formed you, as if you were a season I could
strap myself into and ride like a sled.

Your instincts were whole relics preserved
in stone, the space around you a lair where
you hid in winter. You provided

a subtle gravity, a course through darkness,
unaware that I turned on your axis,
sped like a train in your direction.

I hated your room when Dad was away,
hated sleeping in your double bed.
In '68, when you cruised to Barbados,

I made love on your mattress with a boy
named Pete. We left Rorschachs the size of hands
on your sheets, left the bed unmade.

I look for you everywhere: in the bath,
the mirror, the body of the woman who waits,
there on the platform, like new snow.

THREE VIEWS OF DEATH

"Whatever it was I lost, whatever I wept for
Was a wild, gentle thing, the small dark eyes
Loving me in secret."
— James Wright

1.

A wild gentle thing oozes
from between my legs.
I call him Sam, set up house
around him: the Beatrix Potter,
the portable bar. We rock
in every room, snooze
stuck together like spaghetti.
His soft mouth grips me
in unexpected places.
His skin will never know
the weather of disappointment.

2.

She lurches forward as if
to catch me as I fly
to the ceiling, an "out-of-body"
rising to view the finale.
Behind me, dusk and opaqueness;
below, a busy, funneled scene
with her in the center, seemingly
dead but loving me in secret,
calling me back: "Slip inside me,"
she says, so kindly I float down,
though I don't remember
the floating down, the slipping in.

14

3.

Whatever it was I lost,
I lost between crib bars,
my dark eyes loving you in secret,
my unformed words forming.
You vacuumed noisily up the stairs to my room,
your kerchief sopping with seat,
the second floor of our little rowhouse
steaming in late July heat.
I remember your face, like the moon
between bars, rising
pissed and sullen into my sleep,
and the grinding behind your eyes,
and the suction-sound of the hose
that extended from your body
like the pulsing neck of an angry womb.

CLOISTER

The light of God swings
in the chapel's musk
as if heaven were blowing
through. Far behind me:
the cool black vestibule
of East 28th Street,
the great oak doors barred
shut. No one knows I kneel
before this swaying God,
no one hears what I whisper.
Outside, the poor in flesh sleep
against the old rough wood. My
feet are two lamps, my soles
burn a path to their hearts.
Behind the screen, an old nun
keeps vigil until morning.
Her prayers circle my head.
My naked feet make her cry.

ILLINOIS 80° BELOW

A drunk freezes to death between Cary
& Crystal Lake, slumped inside his jeep
like a rag doll.

He slips his tongue inside my dress, vanishes
like a flame in Chicago wind.

The authorities say he felt nothing,
close the surrounding roads.

It's true: whenever he drinks Coors beer
he cannot be held responsible.

I hunt beneath the linen for the vodka,
wake the next day on the kitchen floor,
body curled in a question.

THE CONTRACT / 1968

His towels
grace the floor.
I run a bath, his brown hair
floats to the top.
I step in puddles, wonder
where to place the blame.
My mother says, "That's
a man for you."
I'm outraged.
There are other atrocities.
"Calm down,"
my parents say,
taking his side.

I am Rosemary
in *Rosemary's Baby*
alone in a phonebooth,
out of dimes.
He looks so sane
in his crisp ironed shirt.
My parents seem so sure.
"You're his wife,"
my father says,
"What did you expect?"
I'm 20 years old,
I whisper. Somebody
help me.

SUMMER SOLSTICE

Meryl Streep & Robert De Niro
are filming at the Dobbs Ferry station.
You catch a glimpse of Streep,
say she's nothing special.

Our baby dies in me, flushed to the river
like ordinary tissue. My head fills
with sea water, my veins
pump the blood of our child.

You become a wall. I beat my hands
against you, fracture every bone.
I can't forget what you said about
Meryl Streep. What did you expect?

This is the week I hate you.
I see the headlines: "Crazy Woman
Murders Yonkers Man" –
not that she meant it. She was
mentally askew, threw herself
on the mercy of the court, off
the Valhalla Dam.

Solstice. You delight me
with tales of Stonehenge, sun
beaming on a single stone.

I love you. Hear the mockingbird
outside our bedroom window? Do we
sound like that?

NINTH MONTH

I grow, circled
by auras: globe
framed in sunlight
and clothed in steam.

You are the moon:
You serve me tea
with toast. Our house
is filled with me.

Whole days float by
in milk. Pungent
dough rises. I
balance, knee-deep,

in breakers, let
my stomach float
as the ocean
rocks my baby.

You are the moon:
You wane as my
body swells, rise
above the sea

and disappear
behind the sun.
The child awakens
while you sleep,

her sorrow bathed in
waves, her ques-
tions old as pearls:
eyes fixed on me.

THE NEW FATHER

He dreams of nothing,
longs to scatter his genes
to the far tiled wall.
He is draped in white,
spectator, cheerleader,
signaling her moves.

He congratulates himself.
She's a good one:
good hips, good pelvis,
good teeth, he adds as a joke.
She bears down,
throws back her head to pant.
The woman in her young eyes
looks past him.
He needs a smoke, shifts
his weight.

The child slides into his life.
"A girl!" they say.
Fear moves in his heart,
darkens his face.
His tears are genuine.

AFTERSHOCK

Had my children awakened
as he spent his rage
on their mother.

Had he slashed the sheets
and punctured my flesh
with his knife.

Had I hoped to love a man,
lie naked beside him, laughing.
Had I died.

Then the death I imagine for him
would be justified,
these voices silenced:

I should have locked the door,
I should have held back the ocean
with my hands.

*

I went down where it was safe,
the first floor
of the dream where

I thought I'd find you.
The moon is in the water, I said,
Everything reflects night.

*

All quakes begin with me,
any rumblings, any split
in dark earth.

Any side glance, any
small slip will do it.
At the core: My fault.

I should have locked the door.
I should have held back the ocean
with my hands.

HUDSON SONNETS

"Dear God! One day she opened
the pantry door and saw
the sea beating among the cupboards,
its webs of brine tangled
like fine white linen
where the cups once were."
— Sandra M. Gilbert,
"Her House," Emily's Bread

1.

Each morning, I serve you three bananas.
They're small, I tell myself, but on their way
to being lethal. Love is always
impatient, unkind. I think of a woman's
life, how long it takes her to write one book.
I think of the black and blues that mark my
knees and chin from walking too fast. Meanwhile
I've stopped touching your face. When I look
in your eyes, I see nothing but fire.
It's Christmas. I buy you a present
because I have to. Lonely or sad,
rosy or blue, love is too intense.
You overwhelm me with your powers.
I'm afraid my own will drive us both mad.

2.

Here we are again, home with the lights fading.
"We'll have a Christmas tree," you say. "A tree
in the house will warm us. Before long we'll be
standing together, loving our tree, loving
each other."
                    Gone the hunter, the captor,
the lust for blood. You're back with your wisdom,
your Windham Hill records, your easy grin.
Inside my headphones I'm frightened or
do I crave the assault of the familiar?
Love hides in shadow like poison arrows,
thirsts for the brush of skin, the hushed voice
of night. I hear Tama drums and wonder:
Will I turn my back on surviving alone?
When you touch me, will I have a choice?

3.

There are fiddles in my head, gentle rhythms
anyone could sleep to, quiet tones
that hurt though they're not supposed to.
You say you love me. I find your arms
too hot, your need deep as a prism
that fractures white light. Am I insane?

I dreamt I died and felt no fear of pain.
Now I fly down the Hudson, duck the Tappan
Zee, head for stations south. The river is
particularly gray. You pushed me out of
bed today, set yourself free. The final sin
is mine. I talked to God, said all this
running drives me crazy. She said: Love
plays a fiddle in your ear. Listen.

4.

Deserted by loved ones during the night,
you'll find yourself the only parade
on this side of the Hudson, displayed
before you: one sharp knife in a pool of light.

This is significant: the light, the knife.
For years I swore you were trying to do
me in with thimbles full of port. You knew
my weaknesses and strengths. Was I right?

A woman with red hair reads quietly while
she eats. The room is empty. The river
flows by as usual. There's an odor
of the past, an echo of ice cubes like
the day we moved from the city upstream
to begin the deliverance of dreams.

5.

The red-haired woman sips wine at a window
table. Presented with salad, she stares
across the Hudson as if saying a prayer.

I myself have rarely been alone.
When I am, I wonder who will touch me,
strain to remember my favorite color,
step carefully as if walking on water.
The river seems to flow beneath my feet.

I imagine carving my initials
on the face of a cliff, rowing downstream
from Ossining to New York harbor where
the Atlantic, splayed with sunlight, hails me.
No memories pursue. The ocean fills
my cheeks with wind, my hair with salt air.

6.

Midnight: I wear gray wool socks, blue jeans
and a cotton shirt the color of pumpkin.
No one can see me. My car is leaning
against a snowbank on 81st Street.
I sit with my back to a picture window
overlooking the park. There are no ghosts here.
I am no longer trembling. My hair
reflects the color of my shirt. It glows
in soft light while you sleep miles up-river
near the hills of Ossining, unaware of my
flight or your freedom. I hear classic
guitars, six of them, while synthesizer
weaves in and out, connecting sounds, fine
threads that cross the air like new music.

THE BELL TOWER

BATYA'S HOUSE

1. Batya's House

Here I am, not working. Batya says:
"How does it feel to be a kid?"
But this is better. This
is Manhattan. My room

is a small sanctuary:
"Mikdosh m'at."
Sheba the Cat dozes on my shell-
pink spread, left ear poised while

Batya stretches in the doorway
like a feline who won't eat meat
or kill a fly. She joins
"Cat lovers against the bomb,"

paints shadows on the sidewalk:
children walking their dogs,
women holding hands,
men crossing against the light.

The summer I sleep here,
New York is a city of white shadows.
At first, I walk around them.
In time, I learn to say their names.

2. 6th Floor

We open all windows from the top,
not the bottom, so Sheba
won't fall out. That means
anything can fly in.

For example, this spider on my arm.
Batya says: "Where did you get *that?*"
I say: "Just blew in." The next day,
there's this turtle in the sink.

"Oh no," Bat says, "Sheba's allergic
to seafood!" And suddenly
there are two sisters playing cards
on my bed. They yell:

"Hi, Mom!" and borrow my clothes.
One sleeps with her foot on my leg,
one reads romance novels all night.
"Who are *they?*" cries Batya.

I shrug. The summer I sleep here,
New York is a city of open windows:
Everything flies in,
everything lands on me.

3. Riverside Park

Three girls smoke pot upwind while
the sun glares white over Jersey.
Every few men, there's one who
thinks he loves me.

"Hey," he beams, "baby, honey, doll."
Is the city safe for women?
I wear my hair short, jeans loose,
running shoes ready for flight,

adopt my best tough face and still . . .
"Mom," prods my fourteen-year-old,
"Ya gotta learn how to drool —
best way to avoid being raped."

I tell her be home by 9 sharp.
I tell her keep a quarter in her shoe.
I teach her how to look, how to run.
I tell her, "If you get in trouble. . . "

She says, "Don't worry, Mom, I'll drool."
The summer I sleep in New York,
we practice at the mirror, Jen and I.
First we drool. Then we learn to spit.

4. Broadway

The little sister sleeps in my t-shirt,
raids my sanctum like a disagreeable twin.
"I hate New York," she pouts,
rudely circles the locals who smile

at her tanned suburban face; makes
Sunday strolls down Broadway seem
like X-rated movies. She decides
to write a poem:

"12 donuts, 12 pizzas, 12 apples,
12 numbers, 12 chapters, 12 steps."
She calls the poem, what else?
Twelve! "12 mommies, 12 daughters. . . "

"Did you know," I tell her,
"that in your lifetime you will deeply touch
at least twelve different people?"
She hugs me, makes me first on the list.

The summer I sleep in New York,
Emily counts stars from the window.
Her eyes peer, dark as mine. Her visions
are echoes of wonder and pain.

5. Pier 88

My tattoo is red with black legs:
a five-day spider from 42nd Street.
I cover it with gauze when I bathe, hope
to prolong its life. My daughter screams

at her first rock concert.
I wait outside, imagine her voice
drowning the rest. The sound
carries me above the river,

above Manhattan Island. Meanwhile,
her father floats by on my left,
captain of MacDonald's blimp.
He says: "Mothers who wear spiders

don't deserve to bake apple pies.
Furthermore, mothers who
spend their time making poems
should be shot down over the Hudson."

The summer I sleep here, New York
offers fruits I've never tasted.
I feed them to my daughters,
one seed at a time.

6. Cathedral

Words rise from the stone floor,
circle sculptures like wind.
I choose a weathered chair, inhale
dust and light from air that

welcomes poets and prisoners,
women-priests, and children
in yellow day-care shirts. I hide
beside a pillar, exhale

endwords to a new sestina while
the sun pours thick blue rays
into my lap, offerings
from the Rose Window.

The summer I sleep here,
New York is a riddle of cool places.
On the hottest days, I search
until each breath becomes a prayer.

7. Brooklyn Bridge

My veins inflate with city air,
my blood hums Manhattan.
I walk into night, ignore the heat,
grow leaner by the minute.

I think about danger: how a woman
learns to sense it, how it rises
with the moon over Brooklyn
and floods the east side of everything.

The city blazes with candles.
Trains inch like jeweled caravans
across the water. The bridge
steals around me, catches me

in a weave of sound and silver.
I straddle Wednesday, Thursday;
July, August. My senses peak
to the level of music.

The summer I sleep in New York,
the ceremonies are of self and severing.
When I die, it will be here,
poised between fear and light.

A SUDDEN LIGHT
IN COLUMBIA HEIGHTS

A sudden light moves along Broadway, uptown
like a low-flying saucer to Freddy's Pizza.
"Whole wheat, extra cheese."
Freddy shields his eyes, extends
a famous steaming slice to the center
of the light's beam.

The West Side rarely stirs at such phenomena.
"Another light," someone says to someone
else. Men fade over their beers, unimpressed,
leering at the usual blondes. The city
yields an orgiastic mob of lights, sirens,
smells. You learn to step around, hold
your breath, wear shades.

An out-of-towner grabs his Nikon FG-20,
fumbles with F-stop and shutter speed,
aims boldly in the light's vicinity, gaping
like the Queens Midtown Tunnel, blinking
like trains beneath the Williamsburg Bridge.
The light cringes, flies down Claremont.

Enrolled at college like any freshman from Flushing
or Los Angeles, the light spends free periods
gleaming over Harlem or roller-skating
down Morningside Drive past the president's house.
Last week it got a haircut on Amsterdam,
the shortest haircut you've ever seen
with a discreet purple streak and the hint
of a tail.

THE KILL

You were startling in your Irish cap, you fox.
I said, Are you a cop?

Your eyes had that Bronson quality,
you leaned against the wall & looked hunted.
I said, Do you dance fast?

You sounded like my sister's ex-fiance
who made her wash his dishes. You answered,
Yeah.

I hurled my secret stones:
I'm older than I look, I said,
I've hairy legs, two kids, & a high I.Q.

I expected a moving target
but you stood so still I kept missing you.

I said, Do you dance slow?
I'm moving to the country in a month —
Joe, what do you say?

You said: Sometimes God is the Hudson River —
whenever life gets crazy
I go down & stick my whole arm in.

CHEAP THEATRICS

We need drama
so after I say he should paint something
you know, more original
and he turns a funny shade of plum
near the classical annex of Tower
Records and drops my hand
and I have thoughts of ego and fears
of driving home with a madman because
by now he's screaming I know nothing
of art, certainly nothing of *his* art
which he thought I loved all these years
but now finds I hated,
I say *goodbye* near Astor Place where
ambulances converge from all over
Manhattan while I squeeze through and down where
there's a man with apricot hair and blood
spurting from his wrist, take the #6
to Grand Central, the 5:50 home
and who do you think is waiting with one
headlight under a full moon and all those stars
with everyone in Tarrytown clapping?

POEM ON THE FIRE ESCAPE

The man I occasionally love sleeps
on the floor in black sweat pants, perhaps
dreaming. I hope so. I blow my hair dry.
It feels like feathers and full of regrets.
I brush them down the drain, imagine them
underground amidst the sludge of Croton,
crawling toward the Hudson that waits, always
in the west, always colder than you think.

I promise myself no more poems
about this man, yet here I am Friday
in the city, chopsticks poised over
broccoli and who walks by? I blend in
with other women, know he won't see me,
his radar characteristically off-
beam. Still, he's driven all the way from Croton
to St. Mark's Place: a coincidence?

Recently, I tried to slip away,
drove as far as the whale tank in Mystic,
stood there until a trooper led me
to a strong pot of coffee. Usually,
I get as far as Manhattan, have this dream:
I lie beside my grandmother, smell
her hops and Viceroys, anticipate
morning and her face: a faithful sun.

The fire escape is visible from here.
My reasons for failure are clear enough,
my reasons for continued flight less clear.
If I hope he awakens, he won't.
If I begin to cross the room, slowly,
so quiet my heart seems to stop beating,
he'll open one eye, and even that small light
will be bright enough to make me stay.

44

THE WOMAN IN THE WINDOW
EATING A WHOLE BLUEFISH

1.

When I close my eyes
I'm in the midst of crickets
on Route 9. Thursday. 3 AM.

I should be sleeping
but quit my job. Again. What
will become of me? Time
turns upside-down. I dream
until noon, awake after midnight
with David Letterman.

2.

I lie beside the bicycles we drew w/ India
Ink at SUNY, Purchase, '83
those first months as lovers.

Now you fish weekends in Pulaski,
a dreary town. And I've begun
to scribble in ballpoint.

What happened to our watercolors?

3.

Sometimes I crave intangibles:
happy children, healthy poems
and sometimes
all the gold I could wear on two arms
would not be enough:
I need a rocket of my own.

Places I'd particularly like to see:
the world, the sun,
Montauk Point.

4.

Our watercolors will be featured on Rock
Video, MTV, Christmas, 1999
in honor of your mother, Bernadette Warholy Skelton
who will be stuffing baked
potatoes, the ones the family loves,
with cheese.

The woman in the window eating a whole bluefish is me.

WOODY ALLEN, WOODY ALLEN

It was the winter of grandmother's
black lamb coat. The wind chill
hit 40 below. *Annie Hall* came to
Manhattan. You called for me
in your white Rabbit, drove me
around the city, froze your tail
on line. You were large, blonde.

The day we married, your acne
flared. We drowned in a foot of snow
outside Mount Kisco.

Grandmother's coat began to shed
in great clumps. I blamed
the tailor, tried to kill myself
with pounds of raisins & mixed nuts.
You jumped impulsively
from a moving car in Barrington, Illinois.
We caught swine flu.

That spring, I said, "Honey?"
You winced. The neighborhood kids
called you names. We sat through *Manhattan*
with strangers, shared the question:
Woody Allen?

47

LETTER TO AN EX-MOTHER-IN-LAW

You died two days before the attack
on Libya. I was grieving over you,
and now this. It's not as if you knew
your leaving would augur war; though back
in '68 you predicted something
might happen over your dead body.
(My marriage to your son?) Actually,
I made this whole story up. Nothing
you said could have offered protection
against the start of a war or the end
of a marriage. Libya seemed a harm-
less shape on the globe. I slept newly armed
with vows and silver trays. You were my friend.
Bombs were slowly turned in our direction.

THE QUESTIONS OF CHILDREN

after a painting by Joan Snyder

I'm a mother myself:
I find lost things, I listen
to invisible friends.

This oil reminds me
of swollen veins and leaking nipples,
mushy pulp and the fruity smells
of sour milk and baby shit.
It makes me cry.

"Why do kids steal pumpkins
from our stoop
and smash them in the street?"

The city's in the seed of Autumn.
A woman floats by on roller skates,
one foot high in the air.
An old drunk wakes and says: "What the hell
was that?" The city smells of pie.

My own mother has one breast left.
She likes to tell the story —
how I rejected her nipple at birth,
how I preferred hard rubber and cold cow's milk.

The pumpkin field stretches, warm
and ripe, along the East Side of Manhattan.
Thick vines connect the fruit,
and seasons flow in circles, bittersweet.

I breast-fed my last child
until her father left me
and I needed a little time.

Now there's plenty of time as
children skate in and out of sleeping drunks,
voicing questions old as cities, cyclic
as Autumn. I tell them: Somewhere
there are plenty of pumpkins.

INVOLVED WITH THIS LIGHT

"What do God and the man who fought
in the Czechoslovakian army and built an
airstrip for UFOs in his backyard have
in common?"
                                    — *my father*

A rare child, age 15, escapes
from rationed smokes and nurses where
she recently locked herself in,
clasping panda and pink toothbrush
beneath her U2 t-shirt, heavy
with music. I receive the call
at dinner and think: This family
has never been dull.

I'm reading Fowles on Wistman's Wood —
a chaos so green it heals —
and Diebenkorn's paintings
from left to right on light
without boundaries. What has my father
to do with God or the man who fought
in the Czechoslovakian army?
He no longer drinks gin
and when he did he almost killed me.

Now he laughs and rents R-rated films
for his grandchildren while
their parents shop unaware at malls,
wonder later at the wide vocabularies
of their baby girls and boys, the way
children slip under without warning.

Before this comfort in chaos,
before Diebenkorn's cities on the brink
of ocean, I often despaired.
As recently as Thursday, while my daughter
hitchhiked home with bear and brush,
I despaired for one brief second,

thinking: What does God have in common
with a man who builds airstrips
for aliens in his backyard?
Thinking: Gin. Picking up Diebenkorn.
Crying salt in the recurring chaos
of doorbell and daughter, thinking: Where
is this light?

TWIN

He prefers county cops: "They'll bust anyone,"
he says, adds: "Local cops suck." He's probably right.
The contradiction, floating on air like a feather,
floats away.
                    Who else,
at two in the morning, on his way to the market
for menthols, and again on his way home,
encounters the Croton village squad car
waiting like a grin in the dark?

Unless it's his new toy:
an old Jaguar, '72, tan —
no heat, though plenty of style and grace —
that inspires the Croton police
to put the heat on him.

It's as if they were bored at two in the morning.
Or perhaps he needed the attention.

Next morning, he's back on his back on the street,
fondling the underside of his car, which looks
embarrassed to be moored in Croton:
oversized art deco, tugboated upstream
from Columbus Avenue.

He's here, sleeping in my house.
I can feel the double bed shift beneath his child-weight.
And I'm hungry.

When did he discover he wasn't a girl?
One day, in the tub, under the bubbles,
his small hand tripped over something attached,
grabbed hold, and it felt pretty good.

Bathed in our underpants, we accepted with grace
the humiliation of our differences, which were,
in fact, only real or not real at night
when the bed shivered
and I knew it had something to do with him.

A brother sets up desires,
erects them like whole armies,
races them like matchbox cars on dusty roads.
                    And so he's here:
gulping coffee and spewing judgments about life.
And he's mostly right, I think, though
radically unaware of the fact. He doesn't care
about the winning, I see, only the architecture
of the game.

Perhaps I was wrong back then, or else I was
precisely right when I backed away from his maneuvers,
which always resembled cold war.
Looking back now, I wonder: If hunger,
which one?

WINTER HOUSE / SUMMER HOUSE

Incredible. I'm never hungry here.
The wallpaper matches the carpet which
matches the drapes and the loveseat which
match the orange walls perfectly. My hair
is never out of place. I never swear
nor leave impressions on the velvet couch.
My shit does not smell. I can eat my lunch
off the kitchen floor, feel secure where
the wine glasses are film-free, the silver
spotless and every room is a separate
ambiance, a four-star rating in warmer
tones, heat hiked to tropical levels. At
thirty-six, there's no place I'd rather
die than here, safe in the home of my mother.

Sitting around in pajamas feels right.
You were wrong, Mom. I still like myself when
my hair is greasy. Notice how patterns
on my naked walls dance in summer light?
Some days I decide not to brush my teeth.
I sketch oranges in a wooden bowl:
one bathes in sunlight, two in shadow.
Their navels point like arrows west, south, east.
I eat the same foods every single day:
brown rice and tahini, Häagen Dazs,
alfalfa sprouts and black cherry yogurt.
Some days I decide not to wash my face.
I don't clean in spring or launder on Monday.
Weekends I practice sloth as a form of art.

THE SONIC BLUE ROOM

I squint from the doorway, leap
across the old shag to my grandmother's bed.
They say it's been snowing in Illinois
since she died, a thick powder
covering the month of April.

If this room were mine, I'd give it
cornflower walls, wood floor, skylight
facing the moon. It would fly to New York
like a DC-10. No more
missing people, feeling split. Joe
would arrive in his room w/fireplace.
I'd lick the soft hair round his navel
until we were both full.

I remember her beaming face when she heard
my voice. I hugged her shoulders, hungry
for childhood. Yet her death was quiet, fast,
800 miles from me. How remarkable
that I missed it. By her own admission,
she loved me best.

JOURNEY

Snow in the midwest: unoccasional,
expansive. I'm bound to make no sense here,
bound between Chicago and New York,
between a baby crying and her father.

My niece plays a video game called Crossbow. Three years old,
she stands on a chair, tells me where to drop the quarter, presses
the start button. She fires into the sky, far above the ghosts
and boulders that hurl toward the three heroes who walk robot-
like through the deserted desert town.

After Hammond, I set my grieving
to the rhythm of the train. The snow
lies behind me like a forgotten giant.
The night is mostly clear, mostly stars.

I hear stories of Sara's father bruising my sister, pushing her
down the stairs; and Sara, who hides beneath her bed, loving them both
with the hunger of children.

My own father is sixty now, softer.
He holds me, says: "Time passes quickly,"
and puts me on the train, his direction
having changed, over the years, to love.

At Crossbow, Sara misses everything in sight. Final score: 0.
"What did I get?" she asks, beaming.
"Zero."
"Oh boy!" she cries.
"Yeah," I say, "Sure is better than nothing."

The snow, as I left Illinois, was loving
everything: branch, twig, eyelash. We drove
through the marvel of suspension, not speaking.
There I was, leaving; there was the snow.

A DIFFERENT LEGEND

for K. B., in memory

The hour Kevin lived, I watched his sister
through the kitchen window, summer
in her eyes, magic waving in the heat.
At the hour's end, when the phone rang
everything froze inside the window frame.
In my mind, she skips toward the door,
not knowing.

"For the leaves were full of children, . . ."

We clasp hands and wander past cracked
headstones, tattered flags of revolution.
We're searching for a landmark,
a familiar surname recently chiseled
in bright marble. Emily
chews a slice of apple, engrossed
in the quiet parade of dates.

". . .hidden excitedly, containing laughter."

We are, after all, in this remarkable
unreality, surrounded by apparitions
and the quiet dust of generations:
Sleepy Hollow, where boundaries
between living and dead are clouded
and legends revered, even today.

Emily places the apple on her brother's
grave, turns her head, and listens.

(quotes from T. S. Eliot's "Burnt Norton.")

STORM STREET

In the yellow and gray dusk of Storm Street
a neighbor boy plots his early death
on a Caldor skateboard of sleek polished steel
with the written invitation: Windrider.
He veers between parked cars, catches fenders
and flips like a cat, every movement
liquid, aggressive; every chance at life
ticked off as if someone were keeping score.
His father works nightshift at the GM plant,
days remodeling stores near the river.
His mother cleans houses for the wealthy,
bends over her kitchen at night, scrubbing.
It seems to the boy that his life is too
long. He can't decide what he misses,
but there's only one dream unfolding:
He sees the headlights of a car as it
rounds the corner. Before struck, he imagines
himself an arrow speeding through wind —
over the car, over the houses that sleep,
locked and uncompromisingly clean.

THREE FOR JAMES WRIGHT

1. The Longings of Ghosts

You arrive on your birthday, relaxed
after years away. I open my eyes
and there you are: December 13th,
Saturday. There's my pile of laundry,
my Electrolux, and you: more
than a good poem in my bookcase. O

fisher, lover of the devout and natural,
what do you long for?

once my brother took a wrong turn
and was lost forever. Are you
the consolation? Don't tease me
with your promise of partnership
or trips to the corner of childhood.

If you are my brother,
your gentleness will be crucial
to my survival. You're here
on trial, the only way I can trust.
We're both angels: We both
have wings and limitations.

2. Snow Poem

I hear the birds calling snow! snow!
Where do they go in snow?
Why can't I see them perched
on rooftops, huddled
on telephone wires in their
black overcoats and old galoshes?

Listen: You can't hear them now.
You'll never see them. They're
white as ghosts. They've flown
backwards toward heaven,
disappearing in their disguises.

3. Heaven

Dust jackets spread themselves
on my bed like luminous bodies.

How I want each one!
How I long for nothing to do.

THANKSGIVING POEM
FOR JAMES WRIGHT

When you were a photo of a man
on horseback, on a farm in Minnesota,
I zipped my green silk sheath
up the back with difficulty
and went out through new snow
to find your grave on the hillside.
My feet were blue with love,
and flowers hid my face
from names that frowned on cracked stone,
names I'd seen crowning
the family china at dinner.
I found you, felled pine, proud
Indian, like my grandfather: smiling
in his retirement. You reminded me

of another Jim, Native-born from Arizona,
who rode his ten-speed bike to visit me
in Rockford, Illinois. When it snowed,
he walked with the determination
of his ancestors, sat quietly
through hours of Mahler, and watched over me
until I fell asleep. He was a doctor
of chemistry, arrested once
for draft evasion, and once
for constructing a bomb
large enough to annihilate Chicago.

My grandfather was a teetotaler
from the island of Manhattan —
stiff as a paper doll in shellac,
a cornhusk caricature of Lincoln.
It was impossible to picture him

slumped between twin beds,
a lifeless Raggedy Andy. His voice
is clearest to me in winter,
carving the turkey, passing out
fresh pennies to his grandchildren,
hating minorities with the bravado
of a true Republican. You would have
laughed and then, forgiven him.

The first time I had sex with a man,
you were setting rhythms to word, filling
my mouth with flowers. He wore
Old Spice and heavy construction boots.
He was honest, they said,
which proved false, but I loved him.
So I let him in one cold night,
with a pitcherful of beer in my belly
and shots of blackberry brandy
ready to slide back up my throat;
with my silk sheath unzipped
halfway down my back
and my stockings soaked with snow
from dancing barefoot down Treno Street.
And I'd do it again for the velvet
of his legs, the waking as if from winter,
the sheer risk of the first poem.

THE BELL TOWER

The white narcissus in pewter
dies reverently on my windowsill.

It echoes the bells of Maryknoll where
Catskills sleep beneath snow in the north
and Manhattan rises in the south.

John and I stare, red-cheeked, our breath
steam, our quiet voices mixed
with the stillness after bells.

We imagine purity: a single seed planted
in earth, the Hudson before civilization,
the word before it is conceived.

The bell tower is locked to outsiders,
but John has the key.

Beneath the steep ladder he buries bulbs
in burlap-covered pots. Sometimes
he forces blooms in deserted sanctuaries

or the stark vestibules of cloisters.
Today he breaks the stem of a narcissus
and places it in my hand. Today,

when he opens the hatch that leads
to the bells, I am bruised by the glory,
I am holy in the frozen air.

TWO RHYMED PAINTINGS
WITH SONNETS

for the artist, Libby Robinson

1. She Came in with the Tide

The woman in the bottle is a genie
of infinite wishes. Her landing
is aquatic and subtle, her port of choice
Elizabeth, New Jersey, where nothing good
has ever washed in before. For days
she presses her nose to smooth green glass
and wonders about creatures without fins
and colors in the distance, of smoke
and brick. Her father works there. Her mother
loves her but lacks power. She imagines
trees as small as fish eggs, the first trees
she's ever seen. She's delighted when
the first sparrow lands and sings, the first
apple drops to the first solid piece of ground.

My hands are not chaste, my mind is not quiet.
When I reach for fruit from the wooden bowl
I eat it, juice on my fingers, hard black seeds
spit carelessly onto waiting earth.
I am a child becoming woman.
I reduce planets to a single ovum.
My mind gives birth to life, pleasures in it.
It's always sexual, always real —
the possibilities, every fraction of time,
ineluctably present in every passage
of perfect egg or bright blood rinsed away.
My hands taste of salt. The noise in my mind
is never gentle, though I wander
in circles, closer and closer to truth.

2. She Went out with the Tide

Every seven days she welcomes love.
The waves take her back to blue caverns
with only hints of terror. Her wishes
have become less sensible in recent years:
buckwheat noodles in pesto, a raft
of carnivals, trips to snowy regions.
They are often for herself, less and less
for the baffling world. There is always salt
on her lips. She inhabits rivers
and fresh pockets of air. Her family
has migrated inland and out of sight,
surrounded now by sky and the illusion
of horizon. She mourns them as others mourn
the dissolution of dreams or poem's end.

In circles, closer and closer to truth,
I wander through gentle noise in my mind,
the taste of salt on my hands. Bright blood
rinses away and the perfect egg
ineluctably passes into present,
every fraction of time a possibility,
always real, sexual. My mind pleasures
in life, gives it birth: a single ovum
enlarged to the size of a planet,
spit carelessly from a restless earth,
hard black seed I eat with my fingers.
I am a woman becoming child.
When the wooden bowl yields its final fruit,
my mind is quiet, my hands are almost chaste.

Maureen Seaton was born in Elizabeth, New Jersey, raised in New York State, and has recently moved to the (slightly saner) Midwest. She is a teacher, healer, mother of three, and lives with the sculptor/carpenter, Lori Anderson. Her second book, *Fear of Subways*, won the Eighth Mountain Press Poetry Prize in 1990.